The Plant Kingdom

WELDON OWEN PTY LTD

Chairman: John Owen
Publisher: Sheena Coupe
Associate Publisher: Lynn Humphries
Managing Editor: Helen Bateman
Design Concept: Sue Rawkins
Senior Designer: Kylie Mulquin
Production Manager: Caroline Webber
Production Assistant: Kylie Lawson

Text: Sharon Dalgleish
Consultant: Dr. Roger Carolin, Former Associate Professor,
Biology Department, University of Sydney
U.S. Editors: Laura Cavaluzzo and Rebecca McEwen

04 03 02 01 00
10 9 8 7 6 5 4 3 2

Published in the United States by
Shortland Publications, Inc.
P.O. Box 6195
Denver, CO 80206-0195

Printed in Singapore.
ISBN: 0-7699-0481-5

CONTENTS

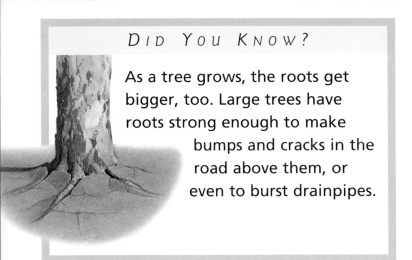

flower

PLANT PARTS

Each part of a plant is important for its survival. Flowering plants have four parts, each with its own special job. The roots hold the plant in the ground and take in water and minerals from the soil. The stem directs the plant toward the light and carries food and water to the rest of the plant. The leaves make food and provide most of the breathing holes for the plant. The flowers make new plants using a female organ, which contains the stigma and the ovary, and male organs called stamens.

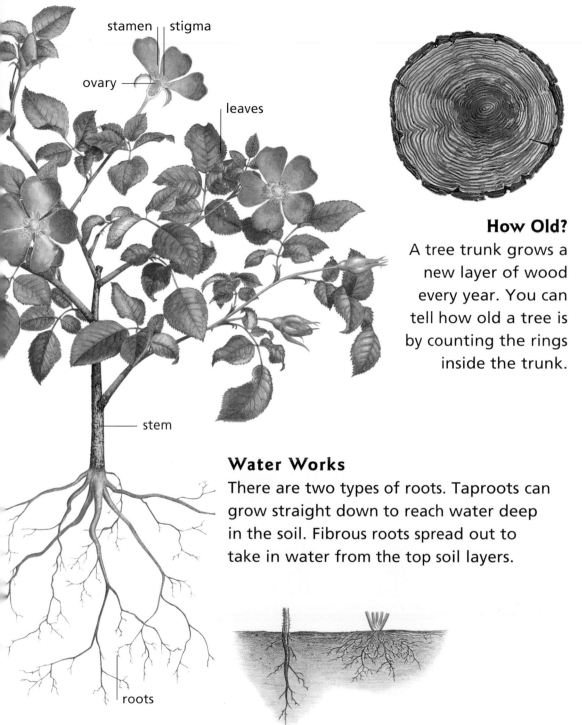

stamen | stigma

ovary

leaves

stem

roots

How Old?

A tree trunk grows a new layer of wood every year. You can tell how old a tree is by counting the rings inside the trunk.

Water Works

There are two types of roots. Taproots can grow straight down to reach water deep in the soil. Fibrous roots spread out to take in water from the top soil layers.

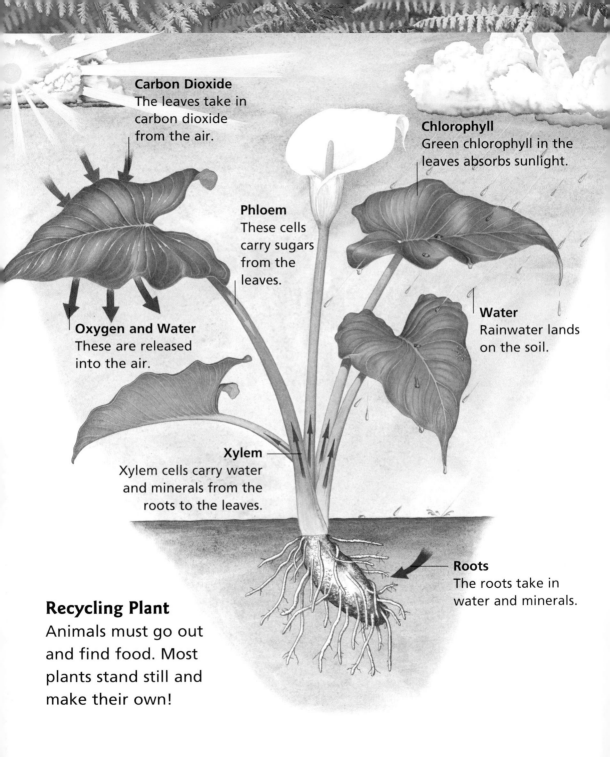

Carbon Dioxide
The leaves take in carbon dioxide from the air.

Chlorophyll
Green chlorophyll in the leaves absorbs sunlight.

Phloem
These cells carry sugars from the leaves.

Oxygen and Water
These are released into the air.

Water
Rainwater lands on the soil.

Xylem
Xylem cells carry water and minerals from the roots to the leaves.

Roots
The roots take in water and minerals.

Recycling Plant
Animals must go out and find food. Most plants stand still and make their own!

Making Food

Have you ever wondered why plants are so green? It's because they're packed with a green pigment called chlorophyll, which traps the energy in sunlight so they can live and grow. They're like green food factories. The whole process is called photosynthesis—*photos* means "daylight" in Greek.

On Vacation
When it isn't flowering, a daffodil rests and stores food in its bulb. This provides energy for new growth.

Fast Growth
Many trees grow quickly in rain forests because there is plenty of sunlight and rain.

SPROUTING SEEDS

Many plants grow from seeds. Some plants scatter their own seeds. Others rely on wind, water, or animals to spread their seeds. A seed needs to find its own patch of ground, away from the shade of its parent plant, before it can sprout a stem and roots. It can wait for days, months, or even years until the conditions are just right, because inside its case it has a handy supply of food.

AMAZING!

Some plants have pods that explode to scatter their seeds, shooting them out at up to 15 yards (14 meters) per second! These desert plants have a slit in the seed capsules to make them explode when it rains.

Washed Ashore
A coconut, with its seed inside, can float many miles from its parent plant.

Helpful Animals

Fruit bats and other animals eat fruit, often without damaging the seeds. The seeds are either thrown away or passed out in the animal's droppings.

Breaking Out

The seed feeds on the coconut milk, then sends out the first stem and root. As the new plant grows stronger, the outer shell breaks open.

Starting Again

The tree will drop its own coconuts, and the sea will wash them away to find their own patch of ground.

MEDICINES FROM PLANTS

By trial and error, early people discovered that plants could cure diseases, heal wounds, or reduce pain. Today, these traditional plant medicines are studied in laboratories. Scientists find the chemical ingredient in the plant and extract or copy it to make drugs. There is still much to learn about using plants for healing. One rain forest may hold cures for thousands of diseases.

Traditional Medicine
Village doctors in traditional cultures grind seeds to make medicine.

Medicine Chest
Ground herbs are sold in markets. Many herbal cures have been used for centuries.

Some early herbalists recorded their discoveries in books called "herbals." In some cultures a shaman, or chief medicine man, passed on the knowledge. These plants are especially helpful, but only if they are used correctly.

Poppy
The milky sap from an opium poppy contains the powerful painkillers morphine and codeine.

Garlic
Garlic can help cure bronchitis and colds. It can also lower cholesterol levels and blood pressure.

Bloodwood Tree
Aboriginal Australians use this red gum to heal wounds, sores, and rashes.

Foxglove
A drug that treats heart patients comes from dried foxglove leaves.

INVADING IMPOSTORS

Mushrooms, molds, and mildews are all species of fungus. Fungi are not really plants. They have no roots, stems, or leaves and no chlorophyll to make their own food. They feed on other plants and animals. Most fungi are made up of special cells that can break down and digest the cells of almost anything, dead or alive. Their own cell walls are more resistant—otherwise they might eat themselves!

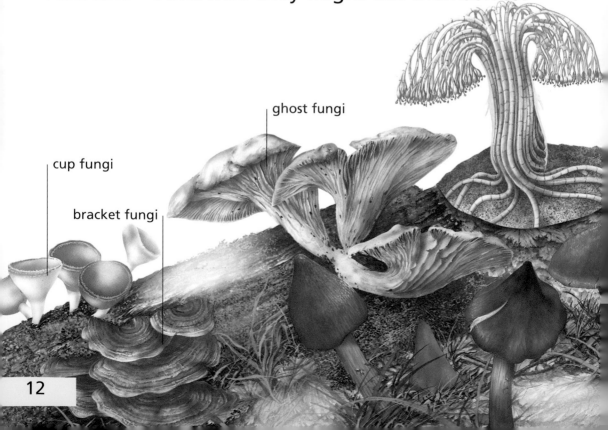

ghost fungi

cup fungi

bracket fungi

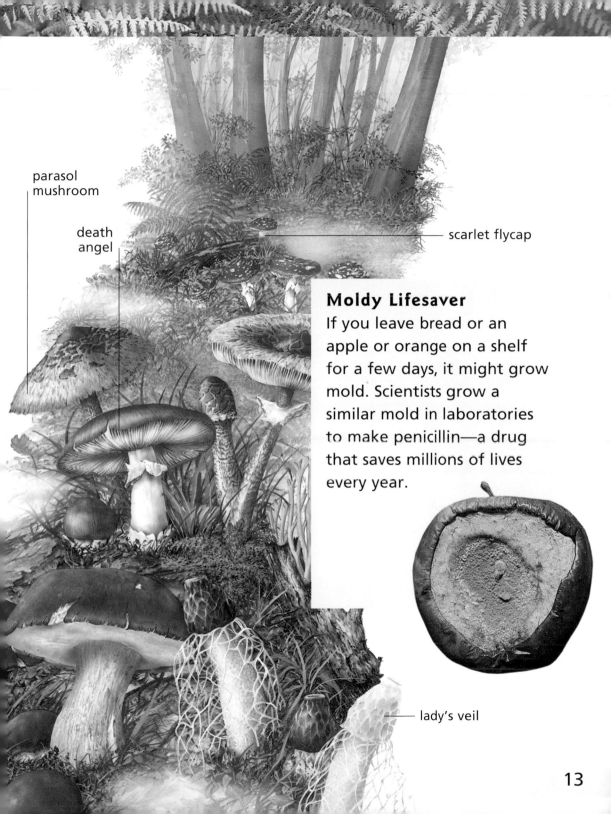

parasol
mushroom

death
angel

scarlet flycap

Moldy Lifesaver

If you leave bread or an apple or orange on a shelf for a few days, it might grow mold. Scientists grow a similar mold in laboratories to make penicillin—a drug that saves millions of lives every year.

lady's veil

13

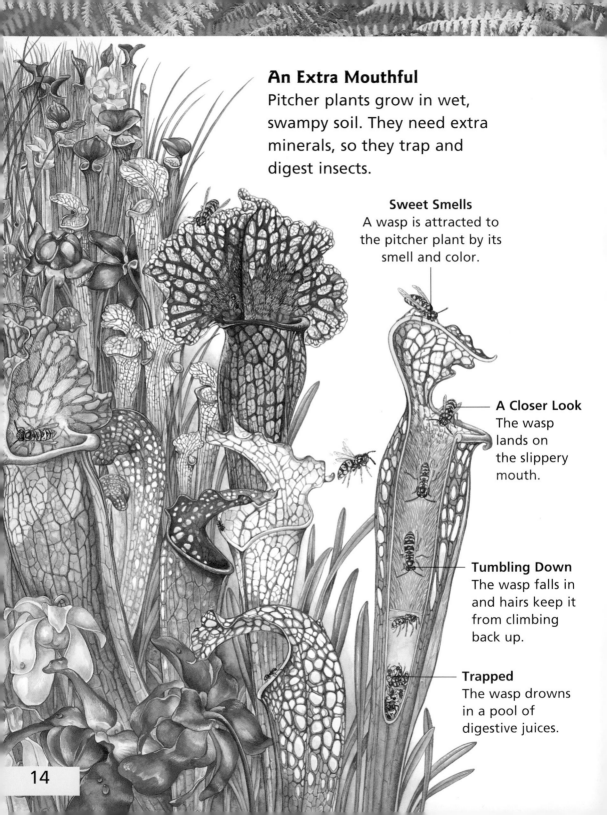

An Extra Mouthful

Pitcher plants grow in wet, swampy soil. They need extra minerals, so they trap and digest insects.

Sweet Smells
A wasp is attracted to the pitcher plant by its smell and color.

A Closer Look
The wasp lands on the slippery mouth.

Tumbling Down
The wasp falls in and hairs keep it from climbing back up.

Trapped
The wasp drowns in a pool of digestive juices.

PLANT ATTACK

Plants can't move around to find the food they need to survive, and they can't run from danger! Instead they have evolved some unusual ways to get extra food and to protect themselves. Some plants can even trap insects and other small animals. Others use scent to attract their prey.

Trapped!
When an insect settles on the inviting surface of a Venus flytrap, it touches special bristles. This sets off a trap, and the leaves quickly close over the insect.

DID YOU KNOW?

In the 15th century, European women used the juice from the deadly nightshade plant as an eyedrop. It made their pupils larger and more beautiful. That's why the plant is also called belladonna—it means "beautiful lady" in Italian.

Taking Over

A strangler fig sprouts from a seed dropped high in a tree by a bird. As it grows, it forms a woody net around the trunk. The tree dies and rots away, leaving the fig to stand alone.

TROPICAL RAIN FORESTS

Tropical rain forests are hot and humid. More plants and animals live in a rain forest than in any other habitat. The leaves of tall trees form a roof of green called a canopy. Some trees grow as tall as 20-story buildings to break through the canopy and reach the sunlight.

Swimming Pool

The tank bromeliad's leaves form a bowl that can collect up to 10½ quarts (10 liters) of water. Many small creatures live in this little world, feeding the plant with their droppings.

Nightlife

Some rainforest flowers keep their petals open at night to attract animals such as insects and bats. These carry pollen from one flower to another, producing the next generation of plants.

Dead or Alive?

This tree may be dead, but it is alive with the activity of other plants, small animals, and fungi.

Rainforest Floor

The rainforest floor is cool, damp, and dark. A layer of dead animal and plant material covers the floor and is broken down by fungi and bacteria. When a tall tree falls, light appears through the space it filled in the canopy. The race is then on for a small seedling to be the first to fill the space.

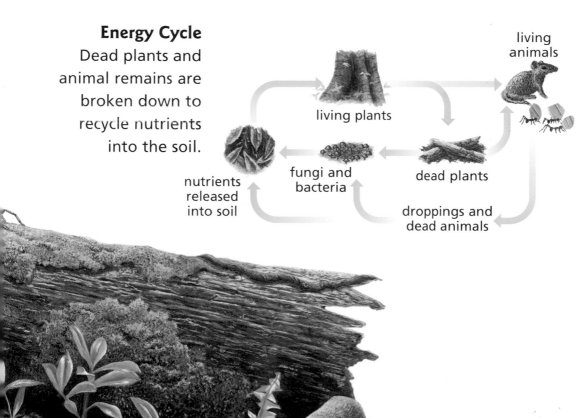

Energy Cycle
Dead plants and animal remains are broken down to recycle nutrients into the soil.

living plants

living animals

nutrients released into soil

fungi and bacteria

dead plants

droppings and dead animals

GRASSLANDS

Grasslands are areas that get more rain than deserts but not as much as forests. Grasses are hardy plants that can withstand dry winds. Many animals graze on grasslands, yet the grass continues to grow. This is because the growing cells of grass are at the bottom of the grass leaf rather than the tip.

A female elephant who has just given birth can eat more than 440 pounds (200 kg) of grass, leaves, and fruit a day. She bulldozes whole trees to find enough dinner.

Grass House
Weaver birds use grass to build safe nests. One tree may hold 400 nests.

21

The puya has a built-in blanket. Its prickly leaves fold up around the stem to keep the plant warm during cold winter nights. No wonder it lives for up to 150 years!

Snow Creeper
Dwarf willows creep along slopes where snow gathers.

Windblown
Lousewort is one of the few alpine plants with a long stem.

Out in the Cold

On high mountaintops, the wind is icy and there is little rain. It is hard for plants to live in this cold habitat. Low-growing plants survive better because it's warmer near the ground. Many plants have hairy stems and leaves to keep water and heat inside. Some even have special sap to keep the plant from freezing solid.

By the Sea

If you stand on a sandy beach and look toward the land, you will see grasses with strong tufts and long, underground stems. They bind the sand and keep it from blowing away. Behind the grasses, the sand dunes are more stable, and roots of low-growing plants take a firm hold. Forests of trees grow in sandy soil beyond the dunes.

From Sand to Forest

Plants on coral islands grow from seeds dropped by birds or carried by the sea. Bare sand can become green forest.

coconut palms   breadfruit trees   beach morning glory

inner lagoon   outer lagoon   channel

patch reef   barrier reef

beach

High Dunes
Coastal wattle grows
along the ground.

High Canopy
The canopy of coastal
banksia trees blocks
the strong
sea breezes.

Low Dunes
Animals eat the fruits
of coastal pigface, a
kind of succulent herb.

Close to the Sea
Beach spinifex traps the
sand and keeps it from
blowing away in the wind.

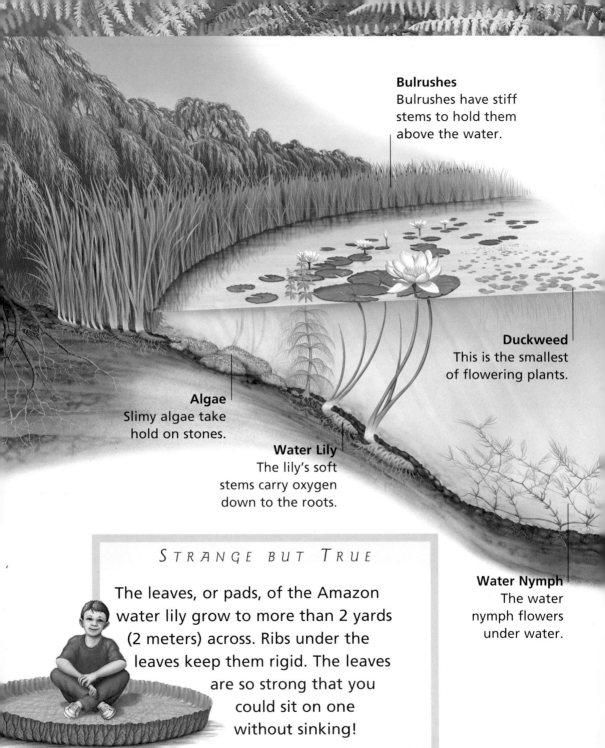

Bulrushes
Bulrushes have stiff stems to hold them above the water.

Duckweed
This is the smallest of flowering plants.

Algae
Slimy algae take hold on stones.

Water Lily
The lily's soft stems carry oxygen down to the roots.

Water Nymph
The water nymph flowers under water.

STRANGE BUT TRUE

The leaves, or pads, of the Amazon water lily grow to more than 2 yards (2 meters) across. Ribs under the leaves keep them rigid. The leaves are so strong that you could sit on one without sinking!

FRESHWATER PLANTS

Freshwater plants grow in the running water of streams and rivers, and in the still, calm waters of ponds and lakes. Some plants float freely on top of the water. Others spend their lives under water, where the sunlight can still reach them. Life looks peaceful for water plants, but their environment can be disturbed by changing water levels and pollution.

From Water to Wetland
Rivers deposit silt when they run into a lake. The lake bed rises and the water becomes less deep. Land plants take root in the silt. Over thousands of years, the lake changes to a wetland.

lake

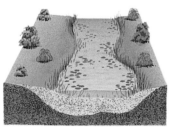

marsh

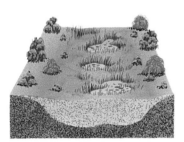

swamp or wetland

In the Desert

It might rain in the desert only once every few years. Some desert plants stay seeds for years, only sprouting when it rains. Desert plants are very good at storing precious water in swollen roots, trunks, or branches. The giant saguaro cactus can store 6 to 9 tons (6–8 tonnes) of water. It provides shelter, safety, food, and water for many desert animals.

Smart Cactus
The flat pads of the beavertail cactus face the afternoon and morning sunlight. When the Sun is high in the sky, the pads turn sideways to avoid the fierce heat.

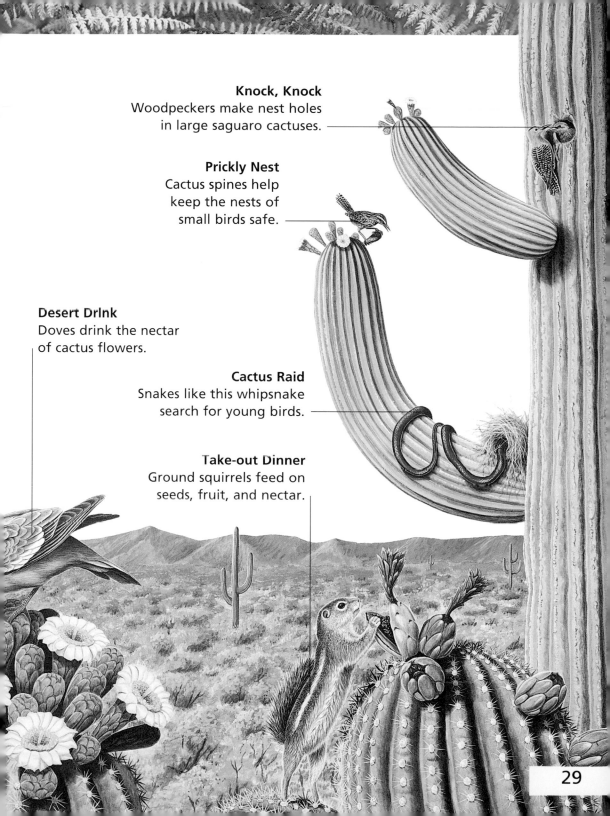

Knock, Knock
Woodpeckers make nest holes
in large saguaro cactuses.

Prickly Nest
Cactus spines help
keep the nests of
small birds safe.

Desert Drink
Doves drink the nectar
of cactus flowers.

Cactus Raid
Snakes like this whipsnake
search for young birds.

Take-out Dinner
Ground squirrels feed on
seeds, fruit, and nectar.

Glossary

canopy A roof formed high above the ground by the leaves of the tall trees in a forest.

carbon dioxide Gas absorbed by plants during photosynthesis (food making).

chlorophyll A green pigment in plant cells that absorbs energy from sunlight to use in photosynthesis (food making).

evolved A description of a plant or animal whose body or habits have gradually changed in ways that allow it to live more successfully in its environment.

habitat The home of a plant or animal.

photosynthesis The process plants use to make their own food.

prey Animals that are caught and eaten by other animals.

sap The juice, made of water, sugars, and minerals, inside the stem of a plant.

silt Earthy matter, such as sand, carried by running water.

stamen The male part of a plant that produces pollen.

stigma The sticky tip of the female part of a flower. It receives the pollen.

INDEX

Credits and Notes

Picture and Illustration Credits

[t=top, b=bottom, l=left, r=right, c=center, F=front, B=back, C=cover, bg=background]

Anne Bowman 22bl, 22c, 28bl. **Bruce Coleman Limited/S. Prato** 13br. **Corel Corporation** 10cl, 21br, 30tc, 4–32 borders, Cbg. **Jon Gittoes** 2tr, 7br, 16bl, 18tl. **David Kirshner** 28–29cr. **David Mackay** 4–5c, 5bc, 6c. **Martin Macrae/FOLIO** 16tl, 16–17rc, 18–19bl, 19cr. **Iain McKellar** 4tl, 8–9rc, 9tl. **Nicola Oram** 8bl, 14cl, 15tr, 15bl, 24bc, FCtr. **The Photo Library, Sydney/S. Fraser/SPL** 10br. **Trevor Ruth** 3br, 20–21c, 21tc, 24–25rc. **Claudia Saraceni** 11tr, 11bc, 11cr, 11cl, FCtl. **Michael Saunders** 5tr, 12–13c, 22tl, 22–23c, BC, FCbc. **Kevin Stead** 1c, 26c, 26br, 27bl, 27bc, 27br. **Ann Winterbotham** 7bl, 31br.

Acknowledgements

Weldon Owen would like to thank the following people for their assistance in the production of this book:
Jocelyne Best, Peta Gorman, Tracey Jackson, Andrew Kelly, Sarah Mattern, Emily Wood.